# AAT Professional Diploma in Accounting

## Level 4

## Financial Statements of Limited

Fifth edition 2020

ISBN 9781 5097 3312 5

**British Library Cataloguing-in-Publication Data**

A catalogue record for this book is available from the British Library

Published by

BPP Learning Media Ltd,
BPP House, Aldine Place,
142-144 Uxbridge Road,
London W12 8AA

www.bpp.com/learningmedia

Printed in the United Kingdom

Your learning materials, published by BPP Learning Media Ltd, are printed on paper obtained from traceable sustainable sources.

Welcome to BPP Learning Media's AAT **Passcards** for **Financial Statements of Limited Companies**.

- They **save you time**. Important topics are summarised for you.
- They incorporate **diagrams** to kick-start your memory.
- They follow the overall **structure** of the BPP Course Book, but BPP's AAT **Passcards** are not just a condensed book. Each card has been separately designed for clear presentation. Topics are self- contained and can be grasped visually.
- AAT **Passcards** are **just the right size** for pockets and bags when studying on the move.
- AAT **Passcards focus on the assessment** you will be facing.
- AAT **Passcards focus on the essential points** that you need to know in the workplace, or when completing your assessment.

Run through the complete set of **Passcards** as often as you can during your final revision period. The day before the assessment, try to go through the **Passcards** again! You will then be well on your way to completing your assessment successfully.

### Good luck!

For reference to the Bibliography of the AAT Financial Statements of Limited Companies Passcards, please go to: www.bpp.com/learning-media/about/bibliographies

## Contents

The BPP **Question Bank** contains activities and assessments that provide invaluable practice in the skills you need to complete this assessment successfully.

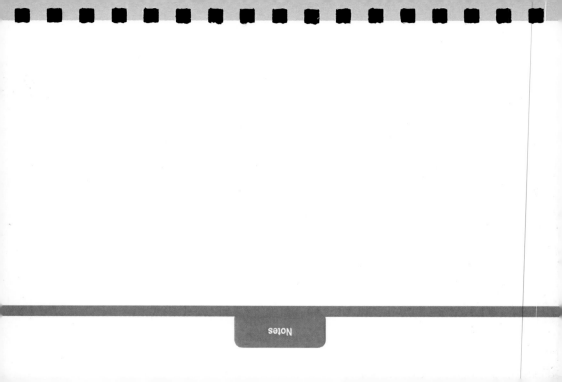

Notes

# 1: Introduction to limited companies

## Topic List

Types of business organisation

The nature of limited companies

The accounts of limited companies

Share capital

Reserves

Loan finance

*The* Financial Statements of Limited Companies *paper is concerned with one specific type of business organisation: the limited company.*

*There are several important ways in which a limited company differs from a sole trader or a partnership.*

## Types of business organisation

There are several broad types of organisation. These can be classified into **profit-making organisations** and **not-for-profit organisations**.

### Not-for-profit

Example:

- Charities, clubs and societies
- Central and local government
- Health services (if government funded)

Aims:

- To provide services to beneficiaries
- To provide services to the public
- To make good use of taxpayers' funds

Economy, efficiency and effectiveness

### Profit-making

Example:

- **Sole traders**: a business owned and managed by one person
- **Partnerships**: a business owned and managed by two or more people
- **Companies**: a business that is a separate legal entity from its owners

Aims:

- Principally to make profits for shareholders
- Other aims are secondary

Your focus is on profit-making organisations, specifically limited companies.

## Limited liability

A limited company gives its owners **limited liability**. The owners' liability is limited to the amount that they have paid for their shares. If the company becomes insolvent, the maximum amount that the owners lose is the amount of capital that they have invested in the company. Investing in a limited company is less risky and therefore more attractive than investing in a partnership or a sole trader. Limited companies may be private (Limited or Ltd) or public (plc).

- Limited companies may be owned and managed by different people.
- Limited companies are owned by shareholders.
- Shareholders appoint directors to manage business on their behalf.
- There may be a large number of shareholders.
- Shareholders receive a share of profit.

The purpose of financial statements is to **provide information about financial position and financial performance to those outside the business**.

- Limited companies must publish their annual accounts (Companies Act 2006).
- These must comply with regulations in the CA 2006 and accounting standards and may have to be audited.

## Statement of profit or loss

Prepared in exactly the same way as for a sole trader/partnership, down to net profit.

|  | £ |
|---|---|
| Revenue | X |
| Cost of sales | (X) |
| Gross profit | X |
| Expenses | (X) |
| Profit/(loss) before tax | X |
| Tax | (X) |
| Profit/(loss) for the period | X |

- Limited companies pay **tax** on their profits.
- This is because a limited company has a separate legal personality from its owners; it is taxed as a separate entity.

## Statement of financial position

Prepared in exactly the same way as for a sole trader/partnership, with exception of capital/owners' interest.

|  | £ |
|---|---|
| Assets | X |
| Equity | |
| Share capital | X |
| Reserves | X |
|  | X |
| Liabilities | X |
|  | X |

## Share capital

Share capital is the capital invested in a company by its owners. The capital of a company is divided into a number of identifiable units, called shares. When a company is formed, it issues shares, which are purchased by investors. Most shares are **ordinary shares**.

- The nominal value of a share (eg £1, 50p) is decided when the shares are issued. Shares are stated in the statement of financial position at their nominal value.
- The market value of a share is the value at which it is traded on the Stock Exchange. This changes over time and is irrelevant to the financial statements.
- Issued share capital is the nominal amount of share capital that has actually been issued to shareholders.

| Ordinary shares | Preference shares |
|---|---|
| ▪ Entitle holders to share in profits (after preference dividend)<br>▪ Entitle holders to vote<br>▪ If the company wound up, entitle holders to any capital remaining after creditors/preference shareholders have been paid<br>▪ Holders are effective owners of company<br>▪ Holders bear risks of business | ▪ Carry right to fixed rate of dividend<br>▪ Do not normally carry voting rights<br>▪ If the company wound up, holders have right to repayment of capital before anything paid to ordinary shareholders<br>▪ Often treated as a non-current liability in the financial statements, rather than as share capital |

## Reserves

- Reserves are part of equity and 'belong' to the equity (ordinary) shareholders.
- All limited companies have at least one reserve: retained earnings.
- Retained earnings = profit made to date, less tax and dividends.

### Distributable reserves

- Can be paid out as dividends
- Include:
  - Retained earnings
  - Other reserves set aside for specific purpose, eg general reserve

### Non-distributable reserves

- Reserves which the company is legally obliged to set up in certain circumstances
- Cannot be used to pay dividends
- Include:
  - Share premium
  - Revaluation reserve

## Dividends

- Profit after tax is available for distribution to the shareholders, in the form of dividends.
- Return on a shareholders' investment; normally expressed as an amount per share.
- Not an expense; therefore not recognised in profit or loss. Instead they are deducted from retained earnings.
- Any profit not distributed as dividends is retained by the company.

## Loan finance

A company can raise finance by borrowing: taking out a long-term bank loan or issuing loan stock (sometimes called loan notes or debentures).

Loan stock and other long-term loans differ from share capital as follows:

- Lenders are creditors; shareholders are owners.
- Interest must be paid regardless of the profit/loss made by the company; dividends need not be paid.
- Lenders can take legal action if their interest not paid/loan not repaid on due date.
- Loans normally have a fixed repayment date.

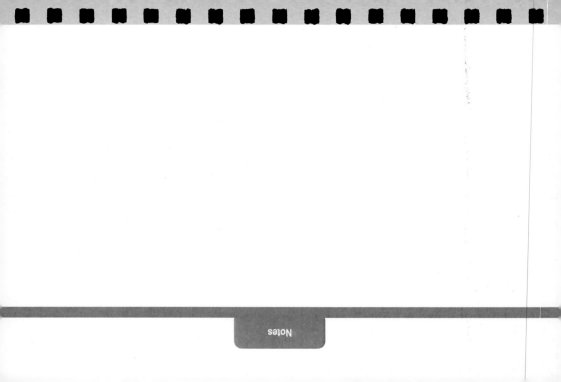

Notes

# 2: The frameworks and ethical principles

## Topic List

The regulatory framework

The IASB's *Conceptual Framework*

Ethical principles

*This chapter looks at the regulatory framework: the requirements of the Companies Act 2006 and the nature of accounting standards.*

*It also covers the IASB's* Conceptual Framework for Financial Reporting.

*Finally, the chapter considers ethical principles, an essential requirement for AAT professionals.*

Limited companies are required to observe various rules and regulations when preparing financial statements. The main sources of regulation in the UK are:

- Companies legislation (the Companies Act 2006)
- Accounting standards

## Requirements of the Companies Act 2006

- The directors must prepare and approve annual accounts and circulate them to the shareholders.
- The accounts must be filed with the Registrar of Companies (ie published).
- Quoted companies must prepare and file IAS accounts (following IFRSs and IASs).
- Other companies prepare either:
    - Companies Act accounts (following UK standards); or
    - IFRS accounts (following IFRSs and IASs).
- Directors have a legal duty to keep adequate accounting records.
- Published accounts must show a **true and fair view** (in IAS 1 *Presentation of Financial Statements* called **fair presentation**).

## Accounting standards

- Authoritative statements of how particular types of transactions and other events should be reflected in financial statements.

- Fair presentation/true and fair view = compliance with accounting standards.

Two sets of accounting standards:

UK accounting standards:
(FRSs and SSAPs)

International accounting standards:
(IFRSs and IASs)

In your assessment, you will be expected to prepare financial statements that comply with
**International Financial Reporting Standards**.

## International Financial Reporting Standards

Since January 2005, all EU quoted companies, including UK companies, have been required to use international financial reporting standards. Two types are in force:

- International Financial Reporting Standards (IFRSs): issued by the International Accounting Standards Board (IASB) since 2001.

- International Accounting Standards (IASs): issued before 2001 by the IASB's predecessor, the International Accounting Standards Committee (IASC).

## The IASB's *Conceptual Framework*

The *Conceptual Framework* sets out the principles and concepts that the IASB believes should underlie the preparation and presentation of financial statements.

It is not an accounting standard.

## Objective of financial statements (general purpose financial reporting)

To **provide financial information** about the reporting entity that is **useful** to **existing and potential investors, lenders and other creditors** in **making decisions** relating to **providing resources** to the entity.

## Users of financial statements (general purpose financial reports)

The *Conceptual Framework* states that the most important (primary) users are:

- Investors (existing and potential)
- Lenders and other creditors (existing and potential)

**Financial statements are prepared in order to give them the information that they need**

Investors and lenders use financial information to make decisions about buying, selling or holding equity and debt instruments, and providing or setting loans and other forms of credit.

They need information about an entity's:

- Economic resources (assets)
- Claims (liabilities) } (financial position)
- Changes in economic resources and claims (financial performance)
- Management's efficiency and effectiveness

## Underlying assumption: going concern

Financial statements are prepared on the assumption that the entity will continue to operate for the foreseeable future; no intention to liquidate or curtail scale of operations materially.

## What makes financial information useful? (Qualitative characteristics)

**Fundamental qualitative characteristics**

Useful information:

- Is **relevant**: it is capable of making a difference in decisions (includes **materiality**).
- **Faithfully represents** what it purports to represent: it is complete, neutral and free from error.
- Neutrality is supported by **prudence**: exercise caution, particularly in areas of judgment and estimates.

**Enhancing qualitative characteristics**

These characteristics enhance the usefulness of information that is relevant and faithfully represented:

- Comparability
- Verifiability
- Timeliness
- Understandability

## Materiality

Information is **material** if omitting, misstating or obscuring it could reasonably be expected to influence the decisions that the primary users of general purpose financial statements make on the basis of those financial statements, which provide financial information about a specific reporting entity.

## Financial statements and the Reporting entity

- A reporting entity is an an entity that is required, or chooses, to prepare financial statements.
- A reporting entity can be part of an entity, a single entity or a group of entities.

## 'Fair presentation/true and fair view'

- Required by CA 2006 and IFRSs
- No definition in IFRSs or *Conceptual Framework*
- 'True and fair' is a legal concept
- Normally given by complying with all applicable regulations, eg IFRSs and IASs
- Meaning changes over time as business and generally accepted accounting practice change

## The elements of financial statements

- **Asset**: a present economic resource **controlled** by the entity as a result of **past events**. An economic resource is a right that has the potential to produce economic benefits.
- **Liability**: a **present obligation** of the entity to transfer an economic resource as a result of **past events**.
- **Equity**: the owners' residual interest in the assets of the entity after deducting all its liabilities.
- **Income**: increases in assets, or decreases in liabilities, that result in increases in equity, **other than** those relating to **contributions from holders of equity claims**.
- **Expenses**: decreases in assets, or increases in liabilities, that result in decreases in equity, **other than those relating to distributions to holders of equity claims**.
- **Contributions from owners**: increases in equity resulting from transfers from owners in their capacity as owners (eg issues of share capital).
- **Distributions to owners**: decreases in equity resulting from transfers to owners in their capacity as owners (eg dividends).

**The elements and the accounting equation**

**ASSETS = EQUITY + LIABILITIES**

**EQUITY = CONTRIBUTIONS FROM OWNERS + INCOME – EXPENSES – DISTRIBUTIONS TO OWNERS**

## Recognising the elements of financial statements

An item that meets the definition of an element (eg an asset or a liability) should be recognised if:

- It is relevant; and
- It will provide users of the financial statements with a **faithful representation** of the entity's transactions.
- An economic impact on the financial statements must be **probable**, otherwise disclose in a note.

## Recognition and the accounting equation

- If net assets increase, income or a gain is recognised; and
- If net assets are reduced or eliminated, an expense or a loss is recognised.

CLOSING NET ASSETS – OPENING NET ASSETS = PROFIT/LOSS FOR THE PERIOD

## Measuring the elements of financial statements

Measurement is the process of determining the monetary amounts at which items are recognised and carried in the financial statements.

Possible measurement bases:

- **Historical cost**: cost at acquisition
- **Current value:** price paid updated for changes in value since acquisition. Can be:

  - **Fair value:** price that would be received to sell an asset or paid to transfer a liability in an orderly transaction between market participants

  - **Value in use:** the present value of the cash flows that an entity expects to derive from the use of an asset and its ultimate disposal

  - **Current cost:** cost if bought today (replacement cost)

Historic cost is the most common way of measuring items, but may be combined with others, eg inventories carried at lower of cost and net realisable value.

Behaviour in society is regulated by the law, rules and regulations, and in some cases by ethical codes.

## AAT Code

The AAT has a Code of Professional Ethics, revised in 2017. The advice for a member is:

- Avoid even the appearance of a conflict of interest
- Be objective and act in the public interest
- Keep sensitive information confidential
- Be straightforward and honest in all dealings
- Maintain professional knowledge, behaviour and skills
- Act within the spirit as well as the letter of the law

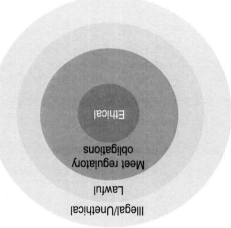

Illegal/Unethical

Lawful

Meet regulatory obligations

Ethical

| **Why should accountants behave ethically?** |
| --- |

- Laws and regulation
- Upholding of professional standards and qualities (personal/professional)
- Protection of the public interest

Enshrined in a 'Code of Ethics' or 'Code of Conduct'

Codes can be     or     Principles and
rules-based to              frameworks to
account for every         guide behaviour
possible situation

## The accountant:

IFAC – international body with its own code of ethics. AAT's is aligned:

F
u
n
d
a
m
e
n
t
a
l
s

- Integrity
- Objectivity
- Professional competence and due care
- Confidentiality
- Professional behaviour

Via: reliability, responsibility, timeliness, courtesy, respect, equality

**THREATS**

- Self-interest
- Self-review
- Advocacy
- Familiarity
- Intimidation

## Professional safeguards

- Entry requirements
- Training requirements
- CPD requirements
- Professional standards
- Professional monitoring
- Disciplinary procedures
- External review

## Importance of independence

Independence promotes:

- Reliability of financial information
- Credibility of financial information
- Value for money of audit
- Credibility of profession

## Safeguards in practice

- Peer review
- Independent consultation
- Partner/staff rotation
- Discussion/disclosure to audit committee
- Reperformance by another firm

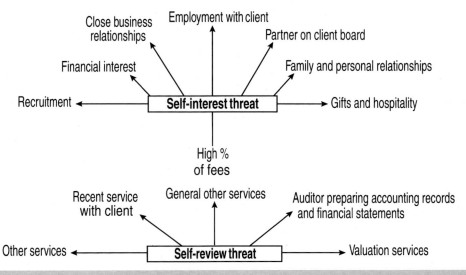

## Advocacy threat

Where accountants take client's part, act as their advocate or will only earn fees from client if successful outcome is achieved (contingent fees). Examples include provision of legal service and corporate finance advice.

## Conflicts of interest

These can arise from accountants acting for clients with whom they are in dispute, eg over quality of work. It can also arise through disputes between two clients for whom accountants are acting.

### Familiarity threat

- Family relationships between client and firm
- Personal relationships between client and firm
- Long association with client
- Recent service with client
- Future employment with client

### Intimidation threat

- Close business relationships
- Family relationships
- Personal relationships
- Staff employed by client
- Litigation

# 3: The statement of financial position

## Topic List

Presentation of financial statements

The statement of financial position

*IAS 1* Presentation of Financial Statements *sets out general requirements for the presentation of financial statements, including the form and structure of the main financial statements.*

*This chapter concentrates on the statement of financial position.*

*Make sure that you practise drafting financial statements; attempt as many assessment tasks as possible.*

## Components of financial statements

IAS 1 states that a complete set of financial statements comprises:

- A statement of financial position as at the end of the period
- A statement of profit or loss and other comprehensive income for the period
- A statement of changes in equity for the period
- A statement of cash flows for the period
- Notes

Financial statements should be prepared at least annually.

## Fair presentation

Financial statements must present fairly the financial position, financial performance and cash flows of an entity. This is achieved by:

- Faithful representation of the effects of transactions/events according to definitions and recognition criteria for assets, liabilities, income and expenses in the *Conceptual Framework*.
- Compliance with IFRSs.

## Accounting principles

### Going concern

Financial statements must be prepared on a going concern basis, unless the entity is not a going concern.

### Accruals

Financial statements must be prepared on the accruals basis, except for cash flow information.

### Materiality and aggregation

- Each material class of similar items must be presented separately.
- Items that are dissimilar must be presented separately. They cannot be aggregated unless they are individually immaterial.

### Offset

Assets and liabilities, and income and expenses, should not be offset unless this is required or permitted by a standard.

### Consistency of presentation

An entity must present and classify items in the same way from one period to the next unless:

- There has been a significant change in the entity's operations; or
- A new IFRS requires a different presentation.

# Format of the statement of financial position

$$ASSETS = EQUITY + LIABILITIES$$

**Statement of financial position as at (date)**

|  | £000 |
|---|---|
| **Assets** | |
| **Non-current assets** | |
| Intangible assets | X |
| Property, plant and equipment | X |
|  | X |
| **Current assets** | |
| Inventories | X |
| Trade and other receivables | X |
| Cash and cash equivalents | X |
|  | X |
| **Total assets** | X |

In the assessment, you will be expected to draft the statement of financial position in a similar format.

The line items should be analysed further, where this is necessary.

Example: property, plant and equipment broken down into:

- Land and buildings
- Plant and machinery
- Motor vehicles

This is normally done in the notes.

**Equity and liabilities**
**Equity**

| | |
|---|---|
| Share capital | X |
| Share premium | X |
| Revaluation reserve | X |
| Retained earnings | X |
| **Total equity** | X |

**Non-current liabilities**

| | |
|---|---|
| Bank loans | X |
| | X |

**Current liabilities**

| | |
|---|---|
| Trade and other payables | X |
| Tax liabilities | X |
| Bank overdrafts and loans | X |
| | X |
| **Total liabilities** | X |
| **Total equity and liabilities** | X |

> IAS 1 specifies the line items to be disclosed.
>
> Present additional line items, headings and subtotals if this helps users to understand the information.

> Classify assets and liabilities as either current or non-current; present these categories separately (see next section for definitions).

## Current and non-current assets and liabilities

These must be classified and presented separately in the statement of financial position.

### Current asset

- Entity expects to receive/sell/consume it in normal operating cycle;
- Held primarily for trading;
- Expected to be realised within 12 months after the year-end; or
- Cash or a cash equivalent.

### Current liability

- Entity expects to settle it in its normal operating cycle;
- Held primarily for trading;
- Due to be settled within 12 months after the year-end; or
- Entity does not have the unconditional right to delay settling it for at least 12 months after the year-end.

**All other assets and liabilities are non-current.**

# 4: The statements of financial performance

## Topic List

The statement of profit or loss and other comprehensive income

The statement of changes in equity

The financial statements

*This chapter concentrates on the statement of profit or loss and other comprehensive income and the statement of changes in equity.*

*As with the statement of financial position, you should practise drafting these statements by attempting as many assessment tasks as possible.*

## Format

**Statement of profit or loss and other comprehensive income for the year ended**

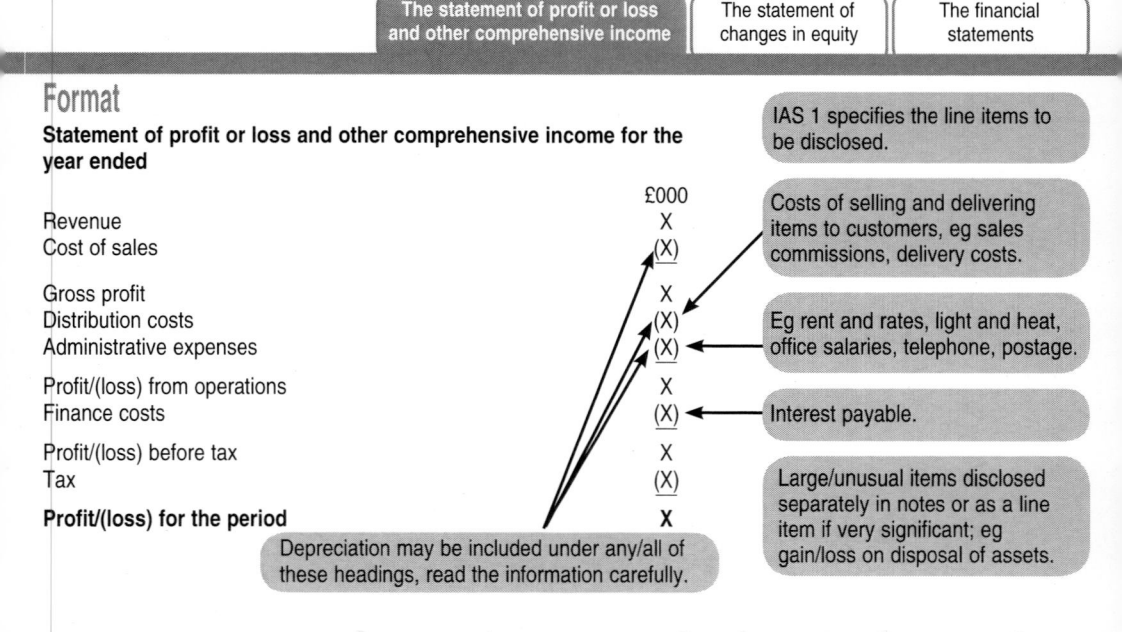

IAS 1 specifies the line items to be disclosed.

| | £000 |
|---|---|
| Revenue | X |
| Cost of sales | (X) |
| | |
| Gross profit | X |
| Distribution costs | (X) |
| Administrative expenses | (X) |
| | |
| Profit/(loss) from operations | X |
| Finance costs | (X) |
| | |
| Profit/(loss) before tax | X |
| Tax | (X) |
| | |
| **Profit/(loss) for the period** | **X** |

Costs of selling and delivering items to customers, eg sales commissions, delivery costs.

Eg rent and rates, light and heat, office salaries, telephone, postage.

Interest payable.

Large/unusual items disclosed separately in notes or as a line item if very significant; eg gain/loss on disposal of assets.

Depreciation may be included under any/all of these headings, read the information carefully.

**Other comprehensive income for the period:**

Gains on property revaluation

**Total comprehensive income for the period**

| | £000 |
|---|---|
| | X |
| | X |

> All items of income and expense for period should be included in profit or loss unless another standard requires otherwise.

> Must be line item for each component of other comprehensive income (only gain/loss on revaluation in assessment).

**In the assessment, you will be asked to draft a single statement of profit or loss and other comprehensive income in a similar format to the one above.**

IAS 1 also allows an entity to present two separate statements:

- A statement of profit or loss; and
- A statement of comprehensive income (showing profit/loss and other comprehensive income).

**4:** The statements of financial performance

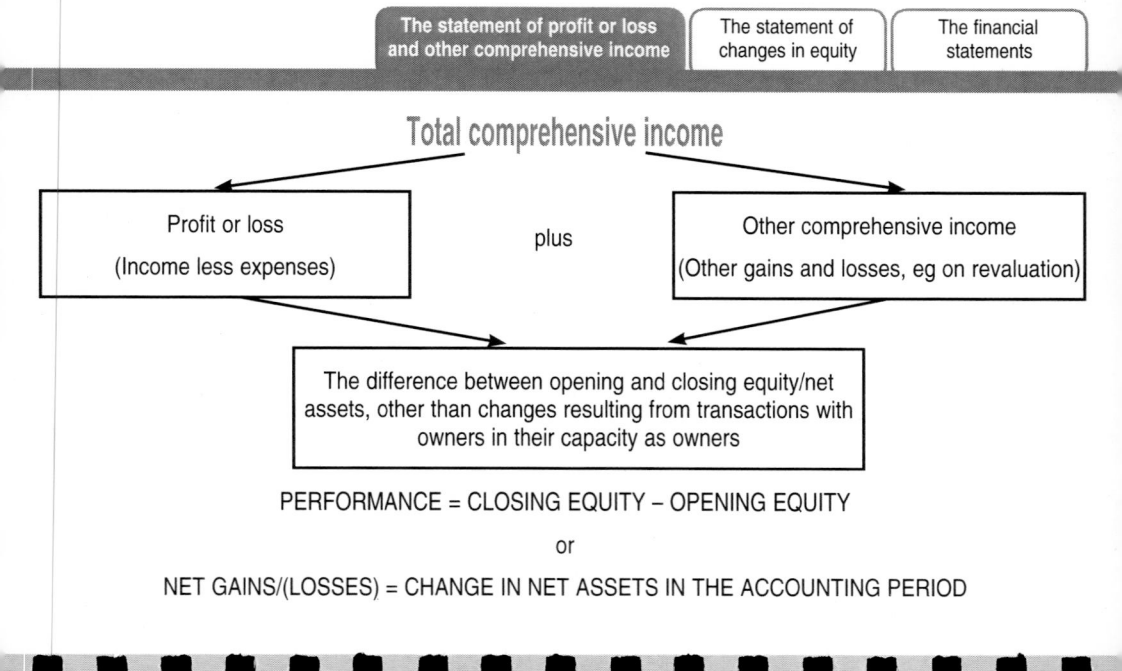

## Example of a statement of changes in equity

**Statement of changes in equity for the year ended**

|  | Share capital | Other reserves | Retained earnings | Total equity |
|---|---|---|---|---|
|  | £000 | £000 | £000 | £000 |
| **Balance at beginning of year** | X | X | X | X |
| **Changes in equity for the year** | | | | |
| Total comprehensive income | | X | X | X |
| Dividends | | | (X) | (X) |
| Issue of share capital | X | X | | X |
| **Balance at end of year** | X | X | X | X |

## The financial statements

| **Statement of financial position at start of year** | **Statement of profit or loss and other comprehensive income for the year** | **Statement of financial position at end of year** |
|---|---|---|
| Assets = | Income – Expenses | Assets = |
| Equity + Liabilities | | Equity + Liabilities |

**Statement of changes in equity for the year**

OPENING **EQUITY** (ASSETS – LIABILITIES) + TOTAL COMPREHENSIVE INCOME + CONTRIBUTIONS FROM OWNERS LESS DISTRIBUTIONS TO OWNERS = CLOSING **EQUITY** (ASSETS – LIABILITIES)

# 5: The statement of cash flows

## Topic List

Requirements of IAS 7

Preparing the statement of cash flows

Usefulness of the statement of cash flows

Interpreting the statement of cash flows

*IAS 7 requires all entities to present a statement of cash flows.*

*In the assessment, there is a good chance that at least one of the tasks will involve drafting a statement of cash flows and a reconciliation of profit from operations to net cash from operating activities. As usual, it is vital that you practise doing this.*

A statement of cash flows summarises all movements of cash into and out of a business during the accounting period. This provides users of the financial statements with information about an entity's ability to generate cash and cash equivalents.

## Definitions

### Cash

Cash on hand and demand deposits.

(Normally includes current account, petty cash, bank overdraft.)

### Cash equivalents

Short-term, highly liquid investments that are readily convertible to known amounts of cash and which are subject to an insignificant risk of changes in value.

(Examples: deposit accounts and investments that mature within three months of acquisition.)

### Cash flows

Inflows and outflows of cash and cash equivalents.

**Cash flows are grouped under headings**

## Operating activities

The principal revenue-producing activities of the entity and other activities that are not investing or financing activities. (IAS 7)

**IAS 7 allows two methods of presenting cash flows from operating activities.**

### Indirect method

Reconcile profit before tax to net cash from operating activities.

Most entities use this method.

### Direct method

List and total actual cash flows.

## Investing activities

The acquisition and disposal of long-term assets and other investments not included in cash equivalents. (IAS 7)

## Financing activities

Activities that result in changes in the size and composition of the contributed equity (share capital) and borrowings of the entity. (IAS 7)

## Format of the statement of cash flows (indirect method)

**Reconciliation of profit from operations to net cash from operating activities for the year ended**

|  | £000 |
|---|---|
| Profit before tax | X |
| Adjustments for: | |
| Finance costs | X |
| Depreciation | X |
| Dividends received | (X) |
| (Gain)/loss on disposal of property, plant and equipment | (X) |
| (Increase)/decrease in inventories | X |
| (Increase)/decrease in trade and other receivables | (X) |
| Increase/(decrease) in trade payables | (X) |
| Cash generated by operations | X |
| Interest paid | (X) |
| Tax paid | (X) |
| **Net cash from operating activities** | X |

**Direct method shows:**

|  | £000 |
|---|---|
| Cash received from customers | X |
| Cash payments to suppliers and employees | (X) |
| Cash generated from operations | X |
| Interest paid | (X) |
| Tax paid | (X) |
| Net cash from operating activities | X |

**Statement of cash flows for the year ended**

|  | £000 | £000 |
|---|---|---|
| **Net cash from operating activities** |  | X |
| **Investing activities** |  |  |
| Purchase of property, plant and equipment | (X) |  |
| Proceeds on disposal of property, plant and equipment | X |  |
| Interest received | X |  |
| Dividends received | X |  |
| **Net cash used in investing activities** |  | (X) |
| **Financing activities** |  |  |
| Proceeds from issue of share capital | X |  |
| Increase in bank loans | X |  |
| Dividends paid | (X) |  |
| **Net cash used in financing activities** |  | (X) |
| **Net increase in cash and cash equivalents** |  | X |
| **Cash and cash equivalents at beginning of year** |  | X |
| **Cash and cash equivalents at end of year** |  | X |

5: The statement of cash flows

| Cash generated from operations | <ul><li>Start with profit before tax</li><li>Add back finance costs. In your assessment, finance costs will always be the same as interest paid</li><li>Add back depreciation</li><li>Deduct dividends received (if any). These should be included in investing activities</li><li>Disposal of assets: add back a loss; deduct a gain</li><li>Deduct increase in inventories/trade receivables (decrease in cash)</li><li>Add back increase in payables (increase in cash)</li></ul> |
|---|---|
| Interest and tax | <ul><li>Interest: if no accruals, interest charge = cash outflow. In your assessment, this will always be the case, though not always in practice</li><li>Tax: if expense = closing payable, cash outflow = opening payable</li><li>Otherwise: opening balance + charge for year − closing balance = cash outflow</li></ul> |
| Investing activities | <ul><li>Calculate purchase of PPE: opening balance − disposals − depreciation − closing balance = cash outflow</li><li>Calculate proceeds on disposal from carrying amount and profit/loss on disposal</li><li>Include dividends received (if any)</li></ul> |
| Financing activities | <ul><li>Cash flow is normally the difference between opening and closing figures in statement of financial position (share capital and share premium, loans)</li><li>Dividends usually given in task; otherwise reconstruct movements in retained earnings</li></ul> |
| Cash and cash equivalents | <ul><li>Net increase/decrease should equal difference between closing and opening figures in statement of financial position</li></ul> |

## Advantages

- Can alert users to liquidity problems

- Shows how well (or badly) profit is converted to cash

- Cash is a matter of fact and not easily manipulated

- Not affected by accounting policies or estimates

- Can help users to predict future cash flows

- Easier to understand than profit for some users

- Standard headings enable users to compare cash flows of different entities

## Limitations

- Cash balances can be manipulated (eg by delaying payment to suppliers)

- It is possible to focus on cash flow at the expense of profit (eg by not replacing plant and equipment); in the long term a business needs both to survive

- Historical information is not necessarily a reliable indicator of future cash flows

## Interpreting the statement of cash flows

- Has cash increased or decreased in the period?
- How material is the increase/decrease in cash compared with the entity's cash balances?
- Does the entity have a positive cash balance or an overdraft?
- Have inventories, receivables and payables increased or decreased?
- Is there enough cash to cover interest, tax and dividends?
- If there has been capital expenditure, where has the cash come from?
- Is debt increasing or decreasing?
- Will the entity be able to pay its debt interest?
- Will the entity be able to repay the debt (if it falls due in the near future)?
- Is the entity likely to need additional long-term finance?

# 6: Property, plant and equipment

## Topic List

Recognition

Measurement

Depreciation and disposals

Disclosure

*In this chapter, we cover the accounting treatment of property, plant and equipment (tangible non-current assets).*

*You will need to be able to make accounting adjustments, particularly for depreciation, revaluations and disposals of property, plant and equipment. You will also need to learn and understand the main requirements of IAS 16 Property, Plant and Equipment.*

## Property, plant and equipment

**Property, plant and equipment** are tangible items that:

- Are held for use in the production or supply of goods or services, for rental to others, or for administrative purposes; and
- Are expected to be used during more than one period

Examples: land, buildings, machinery, computers, motor vehicles and office furniture.

### Subsequent expenditure

Only include in cost of an item if it will probably result in future economic benefit to entity (by improving performance).

**Do not** include servicing costs, eg repairs and maintenance; these are an expense.

### Recognition

Recognise an item only if:

- It is probable that future economic benefits will flow to the entity; and
- The cost of the item can be measured reliably.

### Measurement at recognition

**At cost:**

- Purchase price; plus
- Any further costs **directly attributable** to bringing the item to location and condition necessary for its intended use.

Includes: delivery costs, assembly costs, professional fees (eg legal), cost of testing asset.

**Does not** include: administrative expenses, cost of staff training to use asset.

## Measurement after recognition

Choice between

### Cost model

(Historic) cost less accumulated depreciation and any accumulated impairment losses.

### Revaluation gains

Not normally recognised in profit or loss but part of other comprehensive income.

DEBIT   Cost: fair value – original cost
DEBIT   Accumulated depreciation: total depreciation to date
CREDIT  Revaluation reserve: revalued amount (fair value) – carrying amount based on original cost

### Revaluation losses

Recognise immediately in profit or loss (if asset previously measured at cost).

### Revaluation model

Fair value less any subsequent accumulated depreciation and subsequent impairment losses.

- Fair value: the price that would be received to sell an asset in an orderly transaction between market participants at the measurement date.

- Fair value is normally market value.

- If chosen, must apply to whole class of assets; eg can revalue properties and keep other assets at cost; but cannot revalue some properties and not others.

- Revaluations should be made with sufficient regularity to ensure that carrying amount not materially different from fair value at year-end.

6: Property, plant and equipment

## Depreciation and derecognition

All items of property, plant and equipment must be depreciated over their useful lives. The only exception is land; it normally has an indefinite life.

### Basic rules

- Recognise depreciation charge for each period in profit or loss.
- Allocate the depreciable amount of an asset on a systematic basis over its useful life.
- **Depreciable amount** = cost/fair value – residual amount (ie where an asset has been revalued, charge is based on fair value).
- **Residual amount** is the estimated amount that an entity would currently obtain from disposal at the end of an asset's useful life.
- No depreciation method is prescribed in IAS 16, but it should reflect the pattern in which an asset's future economic benefits are expected to be consumed.

## Review of depreciation charge

At each year-end (as a minimum) review:

- Depreciation method
- Residual value
- Useful life

If change required, treat as **change in accounting estimate**, for example:

- (If method changed) depreciate using new method over remaining useful life.
- (If useful life changed) depreciate carrying amount of asset over revised useful life.

## Disposals and derecognition

Derecognise an item:

- On disposal; or
- When no future economic benefits are expected from its use or disposal.

Gain or loss on disposal/derecognition:

- Calculate as net sale proceeds (if any) less carrying amount (whether based on original cost or on fair value).
- Recognise in profit or loss for period.

TP03-23521-011

| **Disclosure** | **Land and buildings** £000 | **Plant and machinery** £000 | **Motor vehicles** £000 | **Total** £000 | This is a pro-forma note showing information required by IAS 16. |
|---|---|---|---|---|---|
| **Cost (or valuation)** | | | | | |
| At beginning of year | X | X | X | X | |
| Additions | X | X | – | X | |
| Revaluation | X | – | – | X | |
| Disposals | (X) | (X) | (X) | (X) | |
| At end of year | X | X | X | X | Also disclose: |
| **Depreciation** | | | | | |
| At beginning of year | X | X | X | X | ■ Measurement bases (ie cost or fair value) |
| Charge for year | X | X | X | X | |
| Revaluation | (X) | – | – | (X) | |
| Disposals | (X) | (X) | (X) | (X) | ■ Depreciation methods |
| At end of year | X | X | X | X | |
| **Net carrying amount** | | | | | ■ Useful lives |
| At end of year | X | X | X | X | |
| At beginning of year | X | X | X | X | |

# 7: Intangible assets and inventories

## Topic List

Intangible Assets (IAS 38)

Impairment of Assets (IAS 36)

Inventories (IAS 2)

*In this chapter, we cover intangible assets (including research and development expenditure), impairment of assets and inventories.*

# Intangible assets

An **intangible asset** is an identifiable non-monetary asset without physical substance.

Examples: brand names; technical knowledge; licences; patents; publishing titles; trademarks; goodwill; development expenditure.

## General principles

- To be **identifiable**, an asset must either be **separable** from the rest of the business or must arise from **contractual or other legal rights**.
- Recognise an intangible asset only when:
  - Probable that future economic benefits will flow to the entity; and
  - Cost can be measured reliably.
- On initial recognition, measure at **cost** (ie all directly attributable costs necessary to create/produce asset to operate in intended manner).

## Goodwill

If a business has goodwill the value of the business as a whole is greater than the total value of its individual assets and liabilities.

**Internally generated goodwill**

- Goodwill that a business generates over time (eg through reputation, technical know-how of staff etc).

- Never recognised as an asset (IAS 38 *Intangible Assets* forbids); reason: cannot be measured reliably.

**Purchased goodwill**

- Difference between the cost of an acquired entity and the total fair values of its identifiable assets and liabilities.

- Has a cost to the business that acquired it; this is reflected in purchase price.

- Therefore can be measured reliably at the time of purchase transaction.

- Recognise as an asset in statement of financial position.

**See also Chapters 9 and 10 on group accounts.**

IAS 38 also forbids recognition of other internally generated intangible assets: eg brands, mastheads, publishing titles, customer lists.

## Research and development expenditure

### Research

Recognise expense in profit or loss when incurred.

### Development

Recognise an intangible asset (ie capitalise expenditure) if entity can demonstrate that project meets **all six** criteria; otherwise charge to profit or loss when incurred.

- **Technical feasibility** of completing the asset.
- **Intention to complete** the asset.
- **Ability to use or sell** the asset.
- **How** the asset will **generate probable future economic benefits.**
- **Availability of adequate** technical, financial and other **resources** to complete development.
- Ability to **measure reliably** the expenditure attributable to the asset during its development.

## Amortisation and impairment

- Useful life of an intangible asset can be finite or indefinite.
- If finite, amortise over useful life (same principle as depreciation for tangible assets).
- If indefinite, do not amortise, but review at least annually for evidence of impairment (see next section).
- Also review useful life annually; if no longer indefinite, treat change as change in accounting estimate.

# Impairment of assets

**Impairment** is a reduction in the recoverable amount of an asset below its carrying amount.

An **impairment loss** is the amount by which the carrying amount of an asset exceeds its recoverable amount.

**Carry out an impairment review when:**

- Indication that impairment has occurred

Examples:

- Significant decline in asset's market value
- Obsolescence or physical damage
- Significant adverse change in business or market
- Significant change in the way in which asset is used
- Operating losses/net cash outflows for asset expected

**Annual impairment reviews required for:**

- Intangible assets with an indefinite useful life
- Goodwill acquired in a business combination (see Chapter 9)

## Carrying out an impairment review

An asset should be measured
at the **lower** of:

Carrying amount          Recoverable amount

**Higher** of:

Fair value less costs of disposal          Value in use

- **Carrying amount**: amount at which asset is recognised less any accumulated depreciation (amortisation)/accumulated impairment losses.
- **Fair value less costs of disposal**: the price that would be received to sell an asset in an orderly transaction between market participants at the measurement date, less the costs of disposal.
- **Value in use**: the present value of future cash flows expected to be obtained from asset.

- If carrying amount is **greater than** recoverable amount, the asset is impaired
- Carrying amount − recoverable amount = **impairment loss**

7: Intangible assets and inventories

## Accounting for impairment losses

If asset carried at **original cost**:

- Recognise immediately in profit or loss.

If asset has been **revalued** above cost:

- Treat as downward revaluation.
- Recognise in other comprehensive income (set against revaluation surplus).
- If recoverable amount is less than depreciated historic cost, recognise difference in profit or loss.

- Review remaining useful life and revise if necessary.
- Depreciate revised carrying amount over new estimate of remaining useful life.

## Inventories

**Inventories** are assets:

- Held for sale in the ordinary course of business;
- In the process of production for such sale; or
- In the form of materials or supplies to be consumed in the production process or in the rendering of services.

> **Inventories should be measured at the lower of cost and net realisable value.**
>
> Comparison between cost and net realisable value must be made for each individual item, or each group of similar items, not for inventories as a whole.

**Cost** comprises all costs of purchase, costs of conversion and other costs incurred in bringing the inventories to their present location and condition.

**Do not** include: abnormal production costs, administrative overheads, selling costs.

**Net realisable value** is the estimated selling price in the ordinary course of business less the estimated costs of completion; and the estimated costs necessary to make the sale.

## Methods of arriving at purchase cost

- Actual cost (use where items not ordinarily interchangeable)
- First in first out (FIFO)
- ~~Last in first out (LIFO)~~     NOT ALLOWED
- Weighted average cost (AVCO)

Use same method for all inventories having a similar nature and use.

# 8: Further accounting standards

## Topic List

Accounting for Tax (IAS 12)

Leases (IFRS 16)

Provisions, Contingent Liabilities and Contingent Assets (IAS 37)

Events After the Reporting Period (IAS 10)

Revenue (IFRS 15)

*This chapter looks at the accounting treatment of tax in the financial statements.*

*It also covers a number of other topics: accounting for leases; provisions, contingent liabilities and contingent assets; events after the reporting period; and revenue recognition.*

*Make sure that you understand the main principles of each of the accounting standards.*

## Tax expense

**Statement of profit or loss and other comprehensive income**

**The tax expense (in profit or loss) for the year consists of:**

|  | £ |
|---|---|
| Charge for current year | X |
| Adjustment in respect of prior period | X/(X) |
|  | X |

**Statement of financial position (extract)**

|  | £ |
|---|---|
| **Current liabilities:** |  |
| Tax liability | X |

**Charge for current year**: an estimate of the tax payable on profits for the year.

**Adjustment in respect of prior period**: required because the amount that is actually agreed with and paid to HMRC after the year-end is usually different from the estimate.

Unpaid tax is a **current liability**; usually = the estimated charge for the current year in profit or loss.

To recognise the estimated tax charge for the year:

DEBIT    Tax expense (profit or loss)

CREDIT   Tax payable (current liability)

## IFRS 16 *Leases*

IFRS 16 defines a lease as follows:

'A contract, or part of a contract, that conveys the right to use an asset (the underlying asset) for a period of time in exchange for consideration'. (IFRS 16: Appendix A)

## Accounting treatment

### Lease

- Recognise right-of-use asset (measured at present value of future lease payments plus lease payments before start date plus indirect costs plus dismantling costs less incentives received)
- Set up lease liability
- Liability is increased by interest charges on the outstanding liability and reduced by lease payments made
- Statement of financial position
  - Carrying amount of right-of-use asset
  - Lease liability
- Statement of profit or loss
  - Depreciation
  - Finance charge

### Short-term or low-value lease

- Charge rentals on a straight line basis or other systematic basis over lease period
- Statement of financial position
  - Only accruals/prepayments for rentals
- Statement of profit or loss
  - Rental expense

The treatment of short term or low value leases is a optional exemption from the full requirements of the standard.

## Example treatment

Li Co enters into a five-year lease, payments are £2,000 per annum, payable at the beginning of each year.

The interest rate implicit in the lease is 12%.

1. Calculate the lease liability:

   PV of the remaining four lease payments = £6,075

2. Calculate the right-of-use asset:

   | Liability | 6,075 |
   |---|---|
   | Initial payment | 2,000 |
   | Right-of-use asset | 8,075 |

3. End of year 1 liability:

   | Opening bal | 6,075 |
   |---|---|
   | Interest (12%) | 729 |
   | Closing bal | 6,804 |

Note. split between current and non-current

4. Depreciate right-of-use asset over the shorter of the lease term and the useful life.

## Provisions

A **provision** is a liability of uncertain timing or amount (IAS 37 *Provisions, Contingent Liabilities and Contingent Assets*).

A **liability** is a present obligation arising from past events, the settlement of which is expected to result in an outflow of resources embodying economic benefits (IAS 37).

### Recognition

Only recognise a provision when:

- An entity has a **present obligation** as a result of a past event;

- It is **probable** that an outflow of resources embodying economic benefits will be required to settle the obligation; and

- A **reliable** estimate can be made of the **amount** of the obligation.

### Measurement

Measure a provision at the **best estimate** of the expenditure required to **settle the obligation at the year-end**.

## Contingent liability

Definition:

- A **possible obligation** that arises from past events and whose existence will be confirmed only by the occurrence of one or more uncertain future events; or
- A present obligation that is not recognised.

Do not recognise.

Disclose unless the possibility of a transfer of economic benefits to settle it is remote.

## Contingent asset

Definition:

- A **possible asset** that arises from past events and whose existence will be confirmed only by the occurrence of one or more uncertain future events.

Do not recognise.

Disclose if an inflow of economic benefits is probable.

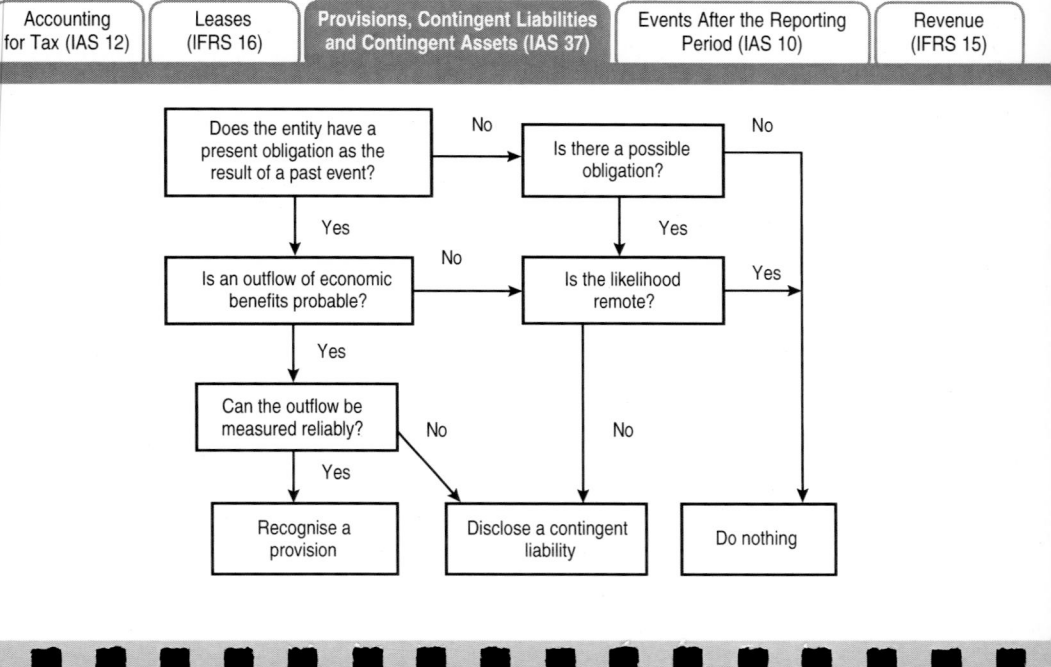

## Events after the reporting period

**Events after the reporting period:** those events, both favourable and unfavourable, which occur between the end of the reporting period and the date on which the financial statements are authorised for issue.

| **Adjusting events:** events which provide evidence of conditions that existed at the end of the reporting period. | **Non adjusting events:** events which are indicative of conditions which arose after the reporting period. |
| --- | --- |

Examples:

- Evidence of impairment of assets
- Insolvency of a customer

Examples:

- Loss of assets due to fire or flood
- Purchase or sale of assets

**Financial statements are prepared on the basis of conditions at the year-end**

**Adjust** the financial statements.

(If material) **disclose** nature of event and an estimate of the financial effect in a note.

## IFRS 15 *Revenue from contracts with customers*

**Revenue** is the income arising in the course of an entity's ordinary activities.　　　　(IFRS 15: Appendix A)

The core principle of IFRS 15 is that revenue is recognised to depict the transfer of goods or services to a customer.

Transfer of goods and services is based upon transfer of **control** over those goods and services.

A contract with a customer contains a promise to transfer goods or services.

This promise is defined in IFRS 15 as a **performance obligation**.

(IFRS 15: IN7)

## Five-step model

The approach to recognising revenue in IFRS 15 can be summarised in five steps.

**Step 1:** Identify the contract with the customer

**Step 2:** Identify the separate performance obligations

**Step 3:** Determine the transaction price

**Step 4:** Allocate the transaction price to the performance obligations

**Step 5:** Recognise revenue when (or as) a performance obligation is satisfied

## Performance obligations

A performance obligation can be satisfied at a **point in time or over time**.

Where a performance obligation is satisfied at a point in time, this will be the point in time at which **control is transferred to the customer**.

Indicators of this are:

- The entity has a right to payment
- The customer has legal title to the asset
- The customer has taken possession of the asset
- Risks and rewards have been transferred
- The customer has accepted the asset

(IFRS 15: paras. 31–38)

### Sale or return

- Where a customer has a right of return, revenue should not be recognised for products expected to be returned.
- Instead, a refund liability should be recognised for the expected returns.
- The inventory cost of items expected to be returned are also excluded from cost of sales and instead remain within inventory.

(IFRS 15 Application Guidance)

# 9: Group accounts: the consolidated statement of financial position

## Topic List

Groups

The consolidated statement of financial position

Intra-group adjustments

*If a company (the parent) controls another company (its subsidiary), it must prepare consolidated financial statements.*

*It is virtually certain that one of the tasks in your assessment will involve drafting either a consolidated statement of financial position, a consolidated statement of profit or loss, or both. Adopt a logical approach and practise as much as possible.*

A **group** of companies consists of a **parent (holding) company** and all its **subsidiaries**.

Although the individual companies within the group are separate legal entities, the parent and the subsidiary operate as a **single economic entity**: the **group**.

## Definitions (IFRS 10)

A **parent** is an entity that controls one or more entities (subsidiaries).

A **subsidiary** is an entity that is **controlled** by another entity (the parent).

**Consolidated financial statements** are the financial statements of a group in which the assets, liabilities, equity, income and expenses of the parent and its subsidiaries are presented as those of a single economic entity.

An investor **controls** an investee when the investor is exposed, or has rights, to variable returns from its involvement with the investee and has the ability to affect those returns through its **power** over the investee.

**An entity is a subsidiary if the parent controls it.**

### Control

An investor controls an investee if and only if the investor has **all** the following:

- **Power** over the investee;
- Exposure, or rights, to **variable returns** from its involvement with the investee; and
- The ability to **use its power** over the investee to **affect the amount** of the investor's returns.

### Power

An investor has **power** over an investee when it has existing **rights** that give it the current ability to direct its relevant activities (usually its normal trading activities).

The most common form of rights that give power are **voting rights** where an investor holds equity shares in another entity.

In the assessment, you can normally assume that control exists where an investor (the parent) owns 50% or more of the voting power of an investee (the subsidiary), unless you are told otherwise.

## Basic consolidation step-by-step

**Step 1**   **Establish the group structure**

> For the purpose of this illustration, we assume that P plc owns 80% of S Ltd

**Step 2**   **Calculate non-controlling interest at acquisition**

|  | £000 | £000 |
|---|---|---|
| Share capital of S Ltd at acquisition | X | |
| Retained earnings of S Ltd at acquisition | X | |
| Fair value adjustments (if any) | X | |
| Net assets at acquisition | | X |
| Net assets × 20% = NCI at acquisition | | X |

**Step 3**   **Calculate goodwill**

|  | £000 |
|---|---|
| Consideration | X |
| Non-controlling interest at acquisition (Step 2) | X |
| Net assets acquired | (X) |
| Impairment of goodwill | (X) |
| | X |

**Goodwill**: an asset representing the future economic benefits arising from other assets acquired in a business combination that are not individually identified and separately recognised (IFRS 3 *Business Combinations*).

- Recognise as an intangible asset in consolidated statement of financial position.
- Measure at cost less any impairment losses (no amortisation).
- Test for impairment annually.

**Step 4** **Calculate the consolidated retained earnings reserve**

|  | £000 | £000 |
|---|---|---|
| P plc |  | X |
| S Ltd: at year-end | X |  |
| Less: at acquisition | (X) |  |
| Group share (80%) | X |  |
|  |  | X |
|  |  | X |
| Less: impairment of goodwill |  | (X) |
|  |  | X |

Consolidated reserves only include S Ltd's post-acquisition profits.

S Ltd's pre-acquisition profits are excluded from the consolidated retained earnings reserve.

**Step 5** **Calculate non-controlling interest at year end**

|  | £000 |
|---|---|
| NCI at acquisition | X |
| Share of post-acquisition retained earnings (from Step 4) | X |
|  | X |

**Non-controlling interest:** the equity in a subsidiary not attributable to the parent (IFRS 3).

In the assessment, it will always be calculated as the portion of S Ltd's net assets **not** owned by P plc.

**Step 6**    Add together the assets and liabilities of P plc and S Ltd

**Consolidated statement of financial position as at (date)**

|  | £000 |
|---|---|
| **ASSETS** | |
| **Non-current assets** | |
| Intangible assets: goodwill | X |
| Other non-current assets (P + 100% S) | X |
|  | X |
| **Current assets** (P + 100% S) | X |
|  | X |
|  | |
| **EQUITY AND LIABILITIES** | |
| **Equity** | |
| Share capital (P only) | X |
| Retained earnings (P + 80% S post-acquisition) | X |
|  | X |
| **Non-controlling interest** (20% S net assets at year-end) | X |
| **Total equity** | X |
| **Total liabilities** (P + 100% S) | X |
|  | X |

The consolidated statement of financial position includes 100% of the subsidiary's individual assets and liabilities. The parent controls 100% of these, even though it only owns 80%.

The sub-total below retained earnings shows the equity that 'belongs' to the parent.

The non-controlling interest in the net assets of the subsidiary is shown on a separate line within equity.

## Fair value adjustments

IFRS 3 states that the identifiable assets and liabilities of a subsidiary that are acquired by a parent should be recognised in the consolidated financial statements at their **fair values** at the date of the acquisition.

- **Fair value** is the price that would be received to sell an asset or paid to transfer a liability in an orderly transaction between market participants at the measurement date.

- The **goodwill calculation** is based on the **fair values** of the subsidiary's **identifiable** net assets **at acquisition date**.

- Therefore, may need to adjust assets to fair value before consolidation (see pro-forma workings above).

- May also need to recognise additional assets/liabilities (eg subsidiary's internally generated intangibles and/or contingent liabilities).

- A gain on a bargain purchase (negative goodwill) is recognised immediately as a **gain** in profit or loss (this is **rare**).

## Intra-group sales

If one group company has sold goods to another at a profit and the goods remain in inventory at the year-end, both inventory and profit are **overstated** from the perspective of the **group**.

- Calculate the amount of unrealised profit
- Adjust the consolidated statement of financial position

**Sales from P to S (P has made profit)**

DEBIT    Consolidated retained earnings

CREDIT   Inventories

**Sales from S to P (S has made profit, so need to apportion between group and NCI)**

DEBIT    Consolidated retained earnings (group share)

DEBIT    Non-controlling interest (NCI share)

CREDIT   Inventories

## Intra-group balances

Cancel out any trade receivables and trade payables against each other.

# 10: Group accounts: further aspects

## Topic List

The consolidated statement of profit or loss

Further points

*This chapter covers the preparation of the consolidated statement of profit or loss. You should pay particular attention to the treatment of intra-group transactions.*

## Basic consolidation step-by-step

**Step 1**    Establish the group structure.

> **For the purpose of this illustration, we assume that P plc owns 80% of S Ltd**

**Step 2**    Add together the statements of the parent and the subsidiary, line by line, from revenue to profit for the year.

- Adjust revenue and cost of sales for any intra-group sales/purchases (see below)

**Step 3**    Calculate non-controlling interest.

$$£000$$

NCI % × S Ltd's profit for the year    $\underline{\underline{X}}$

- If S Ltd has sold goods to P plc during year, need to adjust for any unrealised profit made by S Ltd (see below)

**Consolidated statement of profit or loss for the year ended**

|  | £000 |
|---|---|
| Revenue (P + 100% S – intra-group sales) | X |
| Cost of sales (P + 100% S – intra-group sales + unrealised profit) | (X) |
| Gross profit | X |
| Operating expenses (P + 100% S) | (X) |
| Profit from operations | X |
| Finance costs (P + 100% S) | (X) |
| Profit before tax | X |
| Tax (P + 100% S) | (X) |
| Profit for the period from continuing operations | X |
| Attributable to: |  |
| Equity holders of the parent (P + 80% S profit for year) | X |
| Non-controlling interest (20% S profit for year) | X |
|  | X |

P **controls** 100% of S's results, even though it only owns 80%.

Any impairment loss on goodwill for year normally in administrative expenses.

Profit for the year is split between profits owned by the non-controlling interest and profits owned by the group.

## Intra-group sales

Where one company sells goods to another during the year:

- Intra-group sales and purchases are cancelled against each other; and
- Any unrealised profit is added to cost of sales (it reduces closing inventories).

**To cancel an intra-group sale:**

| DEBIT (reduce) | Revenue |
| --- | --- |
| CREDIT (reduce) | Cost of sales |

by the total amount of the intra-group sale

**To eliminate unrealised profit:**

| Sales from P to S (P has made profit) | Sales from S to P (S has made profit, so need to apportion between group and NCI) |
| --- | --- |
| Increase cost of sales (100% unrealised profit) | Increase cost of sales (100% unrealised profit) |
| | Calculate non-controlling interest as: |
| | NCI% × S profit for the year ..... X |
| | NCI% × unrealised profit ..... (X) |
| | X |

Consolidated financial statements must include **all** subsidiaries of the parent.

Consolidated financial statements must be prepared using uniform accounting policies for similar transactions and other events in similar circumstances.

Must adjust before consolidation if a subsidiary uses different accounting policies from the parent.

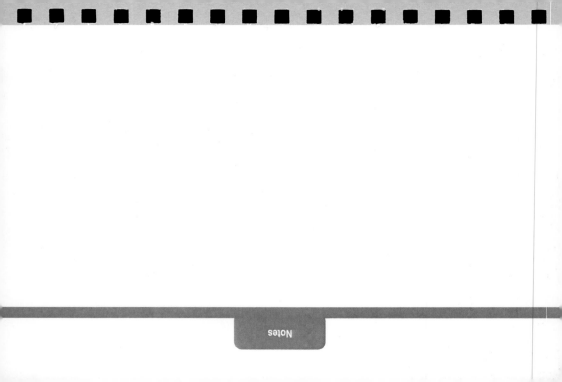

Notes

# 11: Interpreting financial statements

## Topic List

Overview

Profitability

Liquidity and use of resources

Financial position

Limitations of ratio analysis

*This chapter concentrates on ratio analysis, a technique for analysing and interpreting the information in financial statements.*

*As well as learning the calculations, it is essential that you are able to interpret and evaluate changes in the ratios and identify possible reasons for these.*

**The main objective of financial statements is to help users make economic decisions.**

Users external to a business need to interpret its financial statements to understand its financial performance (profitability) and financial position, liquidity and use of resources.

**In the assessment you may be asked to:**

- Calculate ratios
- Compare a set of ratios with:
  - Ratios of the previous accounting period for the same company;
  - Ratios of another company; or
  - Industry average ratios.
- Comment on specific ratios; not only whether a ratio has improved/deteriorated, but possible reasons **why**.
- Suggest ways in which particular ratios could be improved.
- Write a report, letter or email; ask yourself:
  - Who is the interpretation for?
  - What are they most interested in?
  - What decision do they need to make?

## Return on capital employed

$$\text{Return on capital employed (ROCE)} = \frac{\text{Profit from operations}}{\text{Total equity + Non-current liabilties}} \times 100\%$$

ROCE measures the total return made by the company on both loans (debt capital) and share capital. It judges profits earned in relation to the resources available.

ROCE depends on two things:

- Profitability (see operating profit percentage)
- Use of resources/assets (see asset turnover)

$$\frac{\text{Profit from operations}}{\text{Total equity + Non-current liabilties}} = \frac{\text{Profit from operations}}{\text{Revenue}} \times \frac{\text{Revenue}}{\text{Total assets − Current liabilities}}$$

| Overview | **Profitability** | Liquidity and use of resources | Financial position | Limitations of ratio analysis |

## Return on equity

$$\text{Return on equity} = \frac{\text{Profit after tax}}{\text{Total equity}} \times 100\%$$

Measures return to ordinary shareholders on their investment (return on equity only, excluding debt finance)

## Profit percentages and expense ratios

$$\text{Gross profit percentage} = \frac{\text{Gross profit}}{\text{Revenue}} \times 100\%$$

$$\text{Operating profit percentage (net profit margin)} = \frac{\text{Profit from operations}}{\text{Revenue}} \times 100\%$$

Measures the overall profitability of a business

The **expense/revenue percentage** can be calculated for operating expenses in total or for a specific expense:

$$\text{Expense/revenue percentage} = \frac{\text{Operating expenses}}{\text{Revenue}} \text{ or } \frac{\text{Specific expense}}{\text{Revenue}} \times 100\%$$

A high expenses ratio normally = a low operating profit percentage.

## Asset turnover

$$\text{Asset turnover} = \frac{\text{Revenue}}{\text{Total assets} - \text{Current liabilities}} \text{ or } \frac{\text{Revenue}}{\text{Total assets}}$$

Measures the efficiency with which a business uses its resources to generate sales (revenue generated by each £1 of assets). The higher the number, the more efficient the business.

## Liquidity

**Liquidity ratios** show whether a business is likely to be able to meet its debts as they fall due.

| | |
|---|---|
| **Current ratio** $= \dfrac{\text{Current assets}}{\text{Current liabilities}}$ | Shows the extent to which current liabilities are covered by cash or other current assets |
| **Quick ratio** $= \dfrac{\text{Current assets} - \text{Inventories}}{\text{Current liabilities}}$ | Measures immediate solvency of a business. Excludes inventories; these cannot be converted into cash quickly |

The ratios below measure the ability of a business to control its **working capital** and to use it efficiently.

| | |
|---|---|
| Inventory turnover: $$\dfrac{\text{Cost of sales}}{\text{Inventories}}$$ | Shows how rapidly a business's inventories are sold on average during the year |
| Inventory holding period (inventory days): $$\dfrac{\text{Inventories}}{\text{Cost of sales}} \times 365 \text{ days}$$ | Average period for which a business holds an item of inventory |
| Trade receivables collection period: $$\dfrac{\text{Trade receivables}}{\text{Revenue}} \times 365 \text{ days}$$ | Average period taken to collect receivables |
| Trade payables payment period: $$\dfrac{\text{Trade payables}}{\text{Cost of sales}} \times 365 \text{ days}$$ | Average period taken to pay suppliers |

**Working capital cycle** = Inventory days + Receivable days – Payable days

An increase in any of these periods can be a sign of liquidity problems

## Financial position

| | This shows the extent to which a company is financed by debt (loan stock and/or other long term loans) rather than by equity (share capital and reserves). |
|---|---|
| Gearing: $\dfrac{\text{Non-current liabilities}}{\text{Total equity + Non-current liabilities}} \times 100\%$ | This shows the extent to which a company is financed by debt (loan stock and/or other long term loans) rather than by equity (share capital and reserves). |
| Interest cover: $\dfrac{\text{Profit from operations}}{\text{Finance costs}}$ | This shows whether a business is generating enough profit to meet its interest costs comfortably. |

A company with a high gearing ratio often has low interest cover.

High gearing means that there is a greater risk to shareholders:

- Interest payments mean that less profit is available to pay dividends.
- Small changes in the level of operating profit can lead to big changes in the amount of profits available for dividends.

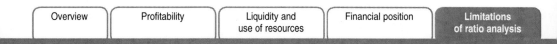

## Main limitations

- Financial statements may be several months out of date.

- Financial statements only include information which can be measured in money terms; items such as intangible assets, human resources and reputation may have a significant effect on performance.

- Comparisons between businesses may be misleading:
    - Different accounting policies
    - Different markets/strategies
    - Effect of size

- Ratios may not always be calculated according to the same formula.

- Ratio analysis may be based on limited information.

11: Interpreting financial statements

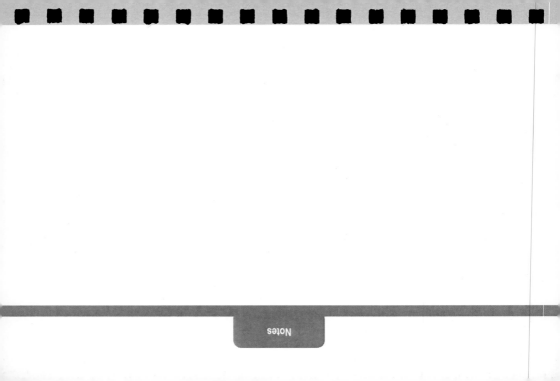

Notes

Notes

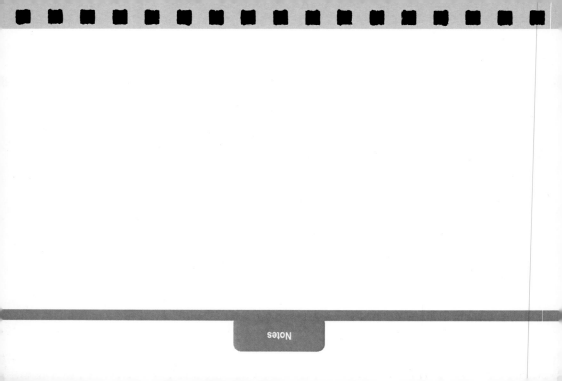

Notes

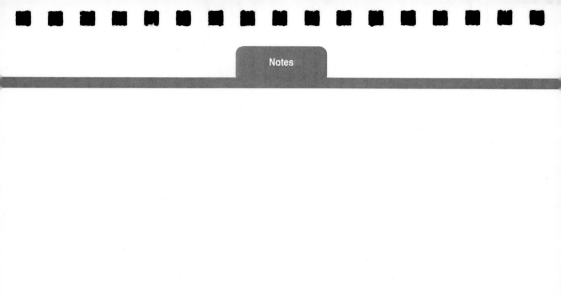

Notes

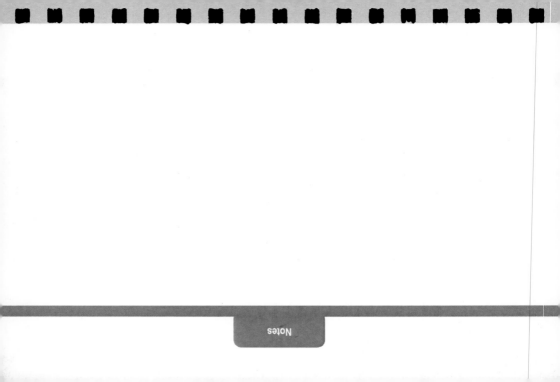

Notes

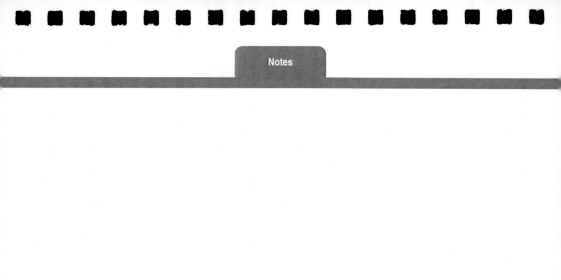

Notes

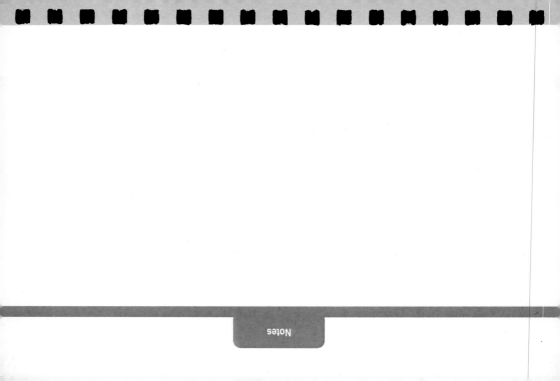

Notes

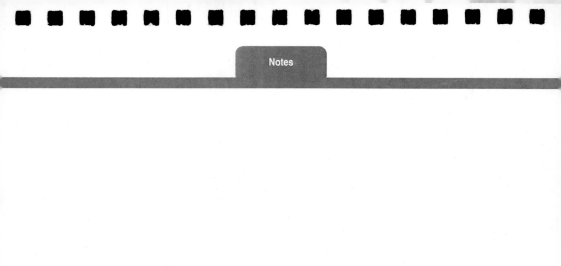

Notes

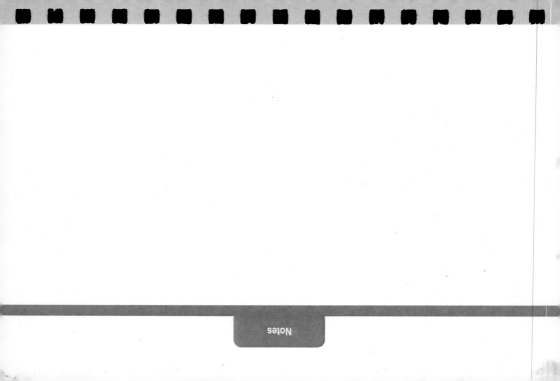

Notes